Shortcuts to

getting a life

Other titles in the series:

Shortcuts to bouncing back from heartbreak
Shortcuts to making hard choices easy
Shortcuts to finding your get up and go (May 02)
Shortcuts to keeping your cool (May 02)
Shortcuts to believing you can do it (May 02)

Shortcuts to getting a life

Gael Lindenfield

Thorsons

Thorsons
An Imprint of HarperCollins*Publishers*
77–85 Fulham Palace Road
Hammersmith, London W6 8JB

The Thorsons website address is: www.thorsons.com

and *Thorsons*
are trademarks of
HarperCollins*Publishers* Ltd

First published by Thorsons 2002

1 3 5 7 9 10 8 6 4 2

A catalogue record of this book is
available from the British Library

ISBN 0-00-710051-5

Printed and bound in Great Britain by
Omnia Books Ltd, Glasgow

To Andalucía

May your 'Mañana' philosophy never die!
You have taught me so much about getting a life.
Thank you.

Acknowledgements for the Shortcuts Series

First, thanks again to all the people who have so openly shared their struggles with me. I hope that you will be pleased that the wisdom I gained from your difficult experiences has been constructively channelled into these Shortcut strategies.

Secondly, many special thanks to Jo Kyle who has done such a magnificent job with the editing of these books. Working with Jo in cyberspace has opened my eyes up to the amazing potential of electronic relationships. I have learned to trust and respect the judgement of someone simply through the exchange of written words. (A good lesson for a writer!)

Thirdly the Thorsons team have been as patient, supportive and willing to experiment as ever. A big thank you to each and every one of you.

Finally, once again my husband Stuart's contribution must be acknowledged. The title of this series was his idea. As ever, I am also grateful to him for his giving over so much of his precious free time to editing my dyslexic manuscripts before they leave the privacy of our home.

Contents

Introduction to the Shortcuts Series

At this moment in your life, reading a book is probably one of the last things you feel like doing. If so, you are exactly the kind of reader I had in mind when I designed this Shortcuts series!

I have struggled with enough personal problems myself to know that when you are in the throes of them, the thought of wading through any book is daunting. You just haven't got the concentration or the motivation. When I am in this situation, all I long for is for someone to tell me what to do – or, even better, relieve me of my hurt or worry by taking it away from me!

So I would like you to think of these Shortcuts guides not so much as books, but as supportive *tools*. I do not intend them to be like an absorbing 'read' to take to the sofa or bath and get 'lost' in. On the contrary, they are designed as 'ready-made' strategies to help kick you into action – and to keep you moving over a period of two months – at least! (Isn't 'the getting going' always the hardest part of solving any problem? This is when I have found that even the most competent and self-reliant people can benefit from support.)

But it is also important that when we do get started, we begin in a *constructive* way. A common mistake is to *do* the first thing that comes into our mind. This can make us feel better because we *feel* more in control. But this 'hit and miss' approach often gets us going on a very much longer and rockier road than we need have taken. In contrast, these Shortcut strategies will guide you along a route that has been meticulously planned. They are derived from years of experimentation and studying other people's tried and tested paths.

The first characteristic of each book that you may notice (and perhaps find initially frustrating) is that they all start with some preparation work. This is because, in my experience, diving headlong into the heart of the problem often proves to be the short-cut to failure!

After you have prepared yourself, the strategy moves along in a series of small steps, each with its own section. Although sometimes these steps will overlap, most of the time you should find that one naturally follows on from the other. At the end of each, you will find a list of tips called 'Action time!' Some of the suggestions and exercises in this section may work better for you than others. But I am confident that in the process of trying them, you are much more likely to find out what *will* help than if you did nothing at all! So I hope you will find them of use one way or another.

Throughout the book you will also find some quotes and key 'messages'. I hope you will find these useful should you just want to dip into the book and gain some quick support and guidance at times when the going feels tough.

Finally, I would like you to always bear in mind that in the personal development field there are no prizes for being first to the winning post. But there are, however, plenty of rewards to be had from the *effective* learning of problem-solving skills. So if you proceed through these Shortcut books at a pace which feels **comfortably challenging,** you will have learned an invaluable skill that could save you time and energy for the rest of your life.

Enjoy the journey! (Yes, problem-solving *can* be highly pleasurable!)

Introduction

'I leave this world without a regret.'

These were Henry David Thoreau's last words.

What an achievement! Who could hope to feel anything better on their deathbed? Although I probably would not wish to have the same lifestyle as this great American experimenter and writer, I know that I would certainly like to feel his sentiments at the end of my life.

But let's not start this book by setting ourselves an impossible target! **If by the end of this book you feel you know how to live a life that will leave you with very few regrets, I'll be happy! And so will you because you will have 'got a life'.**

If that suits you as a good-enough general aim, then this is the book for you.

My guess, however, is that even this muted goal seems more like a dream than a realistic possibility to you right now. If you have picked up this book the chances are that your life is currently quite a struggle. Perhaps you have been feeling powerless to change your situation for quite some time. You could have even been trying hard to accept it. After all, you must know you are not alone. Through my work as a therapist, I have found that there are increasing numbers of people of all ages and all backgrounds feeling similarly even though their life circumstances might appear to be very different. Maybe some of the following sentiments echo some of your feelings:

'I just feel I've "lost the plot" – I don't know what I want anymore. I'm sure everyone looks at me and thinks "she has it all" – the successful, loving husband; an interesting part-time job; two great kids; a bottle of the best Chablis every night; holidays in the Bahamas, etc. I should be happy but the truth is I'm not – I'm bored. Am I just being immature and selfish? Maybe I'm just a spoilt brat having a midlife crisis and I just have to get on with it.'

Janice, a 38-year-old marketing executive

'This is the third job I've had in two years. Each one I thought was going to be the answer at first, but the same thing happens each time – I start okay and then I begin to feel restless. Maybe I just don't like hard work! But seriously, there's got to be more to life than what I've got at the moment – I'm too young to be on a treadmill for the rest of my life. The only thing that I get enthusiastic about nowadays is surfing at the weekends, but I can only get to do that every couple of months now. Perhaps I should forget having a career – my degree [in economics] *doesn't seem to have got me anywhere. I could just chuck it all in and be poor but happy the rest of my life! But I'd never have the guts to do something like that.'*

Mark, a 26-year-old call centre operator

'It's a crazy world now. Here I am sitting at my desk tapping out the prescriptions for Prozac and sleeping pills – and I'm no better myself. I know I'm drinking more than I should, but that's the only way I get to unwind these days. And my partners are just the same – we're all so busy that we hardly pass the time of day with each other. Gone are the days when we used to invite each other for meals or have a drink together or even meet up at conferences. But it's not just the fun that's gone – I think the "heart" has gone out of medicine

for so many of us. It's just become a job that most of us can't wait to retire from.'

Alan, a 53-year-old doctor in General Practice

'Don't talk to me about Monday morning blues – I have those every day. But then who doesn't nowadays? Look around on the underground every morning – who looks happy? And don't talk about my love life – I've resorted to the personal ads but they've been useless. The men I meet through them are only after sex and I'm too tired for that half the time anyway. And I'm getting so unfit. We've got a gym in the basement but I've only got there about half a dozen times in the last six months. Who feels like doing a workout when you leave the office at 1 am? – if you're lucky! All I want to do is crash out at the week-ends so I'm hardly getting to see my friends either. When we do meet it's all one long communal moan anyway. I know it sounds like I earn a lot, but it all gets eaten up in exorbitant London rents and eating out – I haven't the energy to cook a boiled egg these days.'

Fiona, a 33-year-old financial investment advisor

'It was Christmas that did it for me. I'd sweated my guts out going there and the travelling was hell – we spent most of the holiday sitting in traffic jams. I didn't even enjoy the present shopping this year which I usually like.

I was so busy I just ended up getting anything. Next year I can see me doing it all on the internet – not exactly much Christmas spirit in shopping there. And all for what? Everyone sat around in an alcoholic stupor watching the telly. It's not as though I don't love my family, it's just we are all as stressed as each other – we'd be better off eating turkey on our own instead of getting up each other's noses!'

Karen, a 25-year-old nurse

'I leave the house at 6.30 am each morning and am lucky if I get back before 8 at night. I hardly see the children in the week. I am doing the job I always wanted and have a great house with all the trimmings – swimming pool, snooker room, the lot. But the wife and I are constantly bickering. And between you and me, two weeks ago I completely lost it with her – told her I'd had enough. I stormed out and went back to the office and slept the night on the floor of my office. I went back with my tail between my legs and we've been okay since – but it shook me up. That's why I'm here. I know something's going to give. I don't want it to be the marriage or my health. (The last bloke in this job is dead now – heart attack.) But I don't want to chuck in the job – I've put the best years of my life into this company, why should I give it all up?'

Colin, a 42-year-old manager of a chain of clothing stores

'"Harassed housewife" that's how I described myself when someone asked me what I did at my husband's work "do" last Xmas. Of course I meant it as a joke and it was taken as such. But I've been haunted by those words ever since – it's pathetic, isn't it? But that's what I really feel about myself – boring, boring, boring. Although I love the kids to bits and have no regrets about staying home with them – I just feel "Mum" is the only identity I have now. (I remember that's what my dad used to call my mother!) Dave doesn't get home till after eight – we're both so shattered we hardly have two words to say to each other. Weekends just seem to be one continual taxi run – you can't let them go on their own anywhere nowadays – too risky.'

Janice, a 44-year-old mother of two teenagers

Fortunately all these people eventually found another more positive voice deep inside themselves before it was too late. Through doing the kind of self-development work in this book, they have been able to turn their lives around. Some made relatively small adjustments to their schedules and relationships, while others found they had to make much more radical changes. Of course, there are no guarantees that they will continue to live happily ever after, but right now they are much more content with their lifestyles and feel a greater sense of inner peace. And, very importantly, if fate should deal them a negative blow, they now know that they have the 'know-how' to get their lives back on the right track for them.

I hope that there is also a part of you which is saying *'You can do better than count your current blessings'* and *'You deserve more than a third or fourth best crack at life.'* This is the voice that I hope will soon be shouting and screaming in celebration.

And there is absolutely no reason why it shouldn't be if you are prepared to:

a) trust that it *is* possible to have a better kind of life than the one you currently have

and,

b) put in some time and effort over the next two months to achieve it.

But be warned! This book cannot work instant magic. It cannot promise to take your current pain away until a correct 'diagnosis' has been made and a 'treatment plan' set in operation. So it will start in

Stage 1 by showing you how to check that the foundations of your life are as strong and healthy as they need to be. Then in Stage 2 it will take you step-by-step on a 'health-checking' journey through the four key arenas in which our lives are 'played out' – our 'body, mind and spirit'; our personal life; our working life; and our connection with the wider world. As you progress along, it will also give you some suggestions on how you can start making changes in areas that are not working well-enough for *you*.

Work at your own pace

You will notice I have not included specific time guidelines for completing each step. This is because each of you will be working at your own individual pace. Some of you may even want to skip an occasional step or exercise if it is not relevant to you or your lifestyle. As I said earlier, the strategy will take most people around two months to complete if you set aside approximately one to two hours per week to work through the suggestions and exercises. But if you find you need longer, I trust that you will not abandon the strategy just because Mr and Ms Average have managed to work faster than you! (Your life, after all, could be much more fascinatingly complex than theirs!)

What this book will not do is 'prescribe' a better life for you. It may help to think of it as a 'guide' that you may like to have with you on an independent adventurous journey – one that has been written by someone with many years of experience at leading others into these challenging territories. You would therefore expect it to be able to introduce you to a range of well-trodden paths which you may not have discovered yourself, and you would want it also to include many tips passed on from previous travellers.

But you would *not* want or expect it to direct you to one specific destination or give you too exact a route. You would want to remain in full control of your own adventure. And I would assume that you would also wish to be setting your own pace, deciding where and when you wanted to linger and the level of 'risk' you wanted to take.

So are you prepared to set off on this kind of adventurous journey?

Unless you are, it is highly unlikely that you will ever get the 'quality life' I am guessing that you really want. By this, I mean the kind that is both personally satisfying and constructively purposeful (rather than just a brilliant juggling performance with a set of randomly acquired 'balls').

But don't be too daunted. Adventures are about having fun as well as a challenge. And although this Shortcut strategy will be taking you through some uncomfortably confronting territory at times, it has also been designed to act as a support. I have included many suggestions that I hope will boost and build your courage. This is because I believe that courage is the personal quality that, above all others, you will need to live a life without regrets. You will need it to try out different ways of behaving and to experience diverse kinds of relationships. You will need it to stand up for your priorities and to challenge established practices at home, at work and in your community. But most of all, you will need it when you sometimes take the wrong path or someone or something forces you to stop in your planned track and you must find an alternative route. This is the nature of the kind of journey we are setting out on. Living life is inevitably a 'start, stop and start again' excursion. However well we plan and manage it, it will always present us with surprises.

So if you are still up for the adventure, let us begin!

Life is either a daring adventure or nothing at all.

HELEN KELLER

Stage One

the essential foundations

The first stage in our 'getting a life' strategy is the preparation stage. Here we will look at some ways you can create a space in your busy schedule to work through the exercises and suggestions in each step. This kind of work is much too important to try and fit into a few minutes here and there. It deserves an appointment with you on its own! But, in my experience, unless we create this kind of time slot for it, it has a habit of sliding down the priority list. Scheduling it in for some quality time will pay dividends. You will reach your destination faster and enjoy the journey more.

Having done this, we will then look critically at the foundations you will need before you can build a 'quality life'. Until we feel confident that we can meet the basic necessities of life, it is impossible to give the task of finding a happier and more fulfilling lifestyle our full attention.

Life is what happens when you're busy making other plans.

JOHN LENNON

STEP 1

Free up some quality time

Are we putting the cart before the horse?

Yes we are! But we still have to do it. This is because the stark truth is that unless you can create some time to *use* this Shortcut guide, as well as read it, you might as well bin it, or pass it on, now.

This book is about changing your life. That is a task which cannot be achieved without a commitment of time from you. Moreover, it will demand a degree of *quality* time. As I mentioned earlier, **the very minimum amount needed will be one to two hours per week over the next two months**. If you can find more, then your progress will be faster.

Already, I can hear the resistance ringing in my ears:

'If I could create more time, I wouldn't have a problem.'
'I need a 30-hour day to do what I have to do already!'
'I don't control my time – others do.'
'I've already done 56 time management courses and read 300 books on the subject – it won't help!'

These are cries of despair I know so well. Through my work as a therapist, I hear them incessantly from new clients. But, even more importantly, I still hear them in my own head. That's why I can take such a hard line on this front!

I assure you that one of the results of doing the work in this book will be that you will start to find much more time for the life you *really* want. Eventually this will seem to happen easily and naturally – in spite of the obstacles you encounter both externally and internally. But initially this Shortcut strategy will require some kind of sacrifice on your part. The nature of this will undoubtedly vary from reader to reader. For some of you, for instance, in order to find the required time, you will need to give up some money (for example, cut down on some overtime), while for others it may mean risking the goodwill of someone (for example, a colleague or neighbour whom you help out, but who can actually survive without you for a while) or foregoing some pleasure (such as a hobby or watching *every* match) or peace of mind (for example, starting to face the risks that go with making a life change). But whatever you do, it will probably be uncomfortable (change and considering change inevitably is). I guess if you are reading this book, you are hurting already. Feeling disappointed or discontent with our lives is painful, often physically as well as emotionally. So the choice in front of you is not easy. It requires a leap of faith. You must trust not only that this strategy could work, but you must also believe that you can stay motivated enough to persist. Hopefully the following exercises will help you to make up your mind about whether your sacrifice is likely to prove worthwhile, as well as showing you how to free up some quality time to work on this strategy.

Changing your life requires a commitment of time and energy from you. The choice of whether you are worth the investment is yours.

When life is not working for you,
you are being asked to *give up*. Yes!
You are being asked to give up
thoughts, beliefs, perceptions,
habits and fears that hold you back.
There can be no new miracles while
you are holding onto the old stuff.
Pain is a signal to let go, give
something up, open up and try
something new.

ROBERT HOLDEN

Action time!

- **List six things you stand to gain in the long-term from changing your life** (for example, better health / more fun / self-pride) and six things you stand to lose if you don't (for example, your friends / your looks / ten years of your life).

- **Make a list of the 10 main tasks you have to complete during the next month** (excluding work on this strategy for the moment). For example, specific work projects / self-care / care of others / social commitments / house maintenance, and so forth.

- **With the help of your diary, roughly calculate the amount of time you will spend on each of these tasks each day.** Then add all of each task's daily totals to produce some monthly figures.

- **Draw a pie chart** (see page 22 for an example) **or another kind of graphic to illustrate very roughly the proportion of your time each task will take during the next month.** (Using coloured pens will help to bring it to life.)

Reflect on your graphic for 10 minutes or so. Ask yourself:

- is my time being allocated in the way I really want it to be?
- if I were forced to make a choice (for example, by an unexpected illness or a 'hand of fate' emergency) where would I *choose* to make some cuts in these allocations?
- given my current life circumstances, in such a situation, where could I make some cuts with the least hurt, inconvenience and cost?
- is there anyone I could delegate some tasks to to free up some time? (For example, hiring a babysitter / cleaner / gardener, and so forth.)

- **Return to your diary and block out some free periods of time which are left over for working on this strategy** (as I said earlier, this should be at least one to two hours per week). You could give a code name for this 'getting a life' work. (And remember that you don't have to explain this name to *every* prying eye!)

- **Please bear in mind that these 'getting a life' periods need not be set in stone** – they can (and may have to) move around and perhaps be split up – but at least they are now scheduled in. If they do need shifting, the act of doing so will make you think, by bringing the issue we are working on to the forefront of your mind. But if ever you have to cancel and cannot reschedule, be sure to ask yourself if you are (or anyone else is) sabotaging your chances of getting the life you want and deserve.

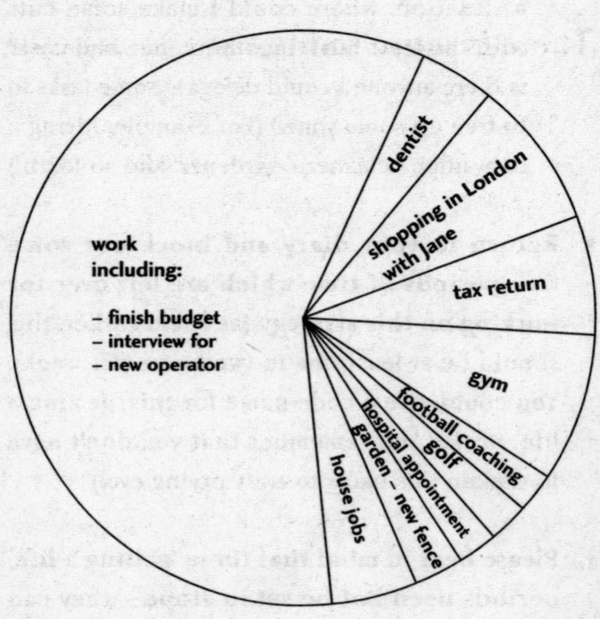

There is more to life than its speed.

GANDHI

STEP 2

Re-evaluate your survival needs

It is certain that unless your fundamental human needs are being met, you will neither have the energy nor the motivation to give yourself the quality of life you are seeking. So you are now going to check how well you are currently meeting these basic requirements for yourself and any dependants you may have.

But be warned – we are not going to be lingering on this step for long!

Why? Because, in my experience, people who are struggling to 'get a life' find it all too easy to get stuck here! Indeed, there is a danger that you could spend a lifetime digging deeper and deeper foundations for your life and never surface to build (let alone live!) the dream you want.

What really are the essentials of life for most human beings today? What do we need to feel confident that we are secure before we set about getting some of our other higher needs (such as social stimulation and support) and wishes (such as more adventure or a faster car) met?

When building the foundations for a life of quality, there are four main areas we have to consider:

1. **Our larder** – it must be full enough to ensure that we and our dependants will not die of thirst or hunger

2. **Our nest** – this needs to be comfortable and strong enough to give us adequate rest and shelter

3. **Our clothing** – this must be warm enough to keep us alive and healthy and also appropriate enough for us to secure our living

4. **Our environment** – we need to live and work in a place which is safe enough not to threaten our survival and be rich enough in resources to allow us to satisfy our other three basic needs.

Men for the sake of getting a living forget to live.

MARGARET FULLER

I hope it is reasonable to assume that anyone who has picked up this book and is sparing the time to read it, is already privileged in all four of these areas. I am therefore presupposing that you do have the ability and means to meet all the above needs to a *good-enough* standard.

But, you may well ask, '*What do you mean by a "good-enough" standard?*'

I believe that if we are honest with ourselves we all know the answer to this question. A much more interesting and relevant question is the one which usually lies behind it: '*Why can't I accept that "good enough" is "good enough"?*' Like so many people, you are probably chasing your tail to secure 'extras' and 'luxuries' which you believe are essential. (For example, the latest fashions, décor and machines / meals in restaurants / holidays abroad, and so forth.)

The simple answer for most people I meet is that they cannot accept that good enough is good enough because they are not in the driving seat of their own lives.

Poverty is not the absence of goods, but rather the overabundance of desire.

PLATO

Here are just a few influences which could be currently 'pulling your strings' and stopping you from accepting that you already have enough of the basics to be able to survive.

- **genes:** these have randomly established a set of pre-programmed responses in your subconscious mind
- **attitudes and beliefs of significant others**: your parents, parent figures, family, friends, boss and influential 'trend setters'
- **memories**: your past experience of life which established fears and set expectations which may no longer be relevant to your circumstances and needs today
- **habits**: the behaviour patterns which you repeatedly use which were trained into your 'personality' by role-modelling or enforced repetition
- **media 'messages'**: values and beliefs embedded in books, music, TV, films or the theatre that you have read, heard or watched
- **advertising**: subliminal and overt messages suggesting that you and your lifestyle are inadequate.

Quite a mixture! And not necessarily one that blends very well together!

The following exercises will help your conscious adult mind to decide which foundations you really do need before you start to build your dream life.

Reassuring yourself that you *can* meet the basic necessities of life will boost your confidence and make it easier to start building your dream life.

Wealth is what you can live without.

JOHN-ROGER AND PETER McWILLIAMS

Action time!

In order to make sure that you have full access to your thinking powers, you may need to rest up first! So find a quiet space where you can concentrate and where your 'strings' are unlikely to be pulled by others' 'essential' needs!

- **Find a calculator** (unless, unlike me, you have one in your head!). Use it to help you **work out how much money you need to keep you and any dependants you have in *adequate* food for the next five years.** Add a reasonably generous amount for factors like inflation.

- **Do the same calculation for clothing.** You can allow yourself some 'treats', such as the odd pair of designer trainers, a posh frock or a hand-finished suit, if those are the kinds of 'must-haves' that you currently crave.

- **Take a hard look at your accommodation and ask yourself if it is currently comfortable enough to provide you with a good-enough place to rest for the next five years.** If not, calculate how much it will cost to make it so. Once again, the odd extravagance is permissible!

- **Ask yourself if your environment is presenting, or is likely to present, any foreseeable major hazards in the next five years?** For example, if you live in an area likely to flood or suffer an earthquake or you live in a politically inflamed society, it would be reasonable to try to set aside resources to cover such contingencies.

- **Review your insurance policies** and ensure that you are adequately covered to meet all these needs should you encounter a major setback such as ill-health or redundancy.

- **Make a contingency plan for any lifestyle changes you may need to make should you encounter a sudden drop in income**. Include how you would research other sources of income to meet your basic needs.

- **Calculate the amount of income you are likely to have over the next five years.** Assess honestly whether or not it is reasonable to assume that it will give you enough to meet your basic needs.

- **If your answer is 'Yes' – read on,** but promise to stop worrying about your survival needs while you are doing so! If you think you can't do this very easily, write out on six cards this statement: *'The foundations are good enough – get a life!'* Place them strategically where your subconscious will frequently get the message (for example, the kitchen cupboard / a screen saver on your computer / the dashboard of your car).

- **If your answer is 'No' – this may be the wrong book for you at *this* moment in your life.** You are likely to be too anxious about these basics to make the best use of it. However, if you feel that it could motivate you to build your foundations even more quickly and securely so that you too can forget them for a while, please do stay with us!

Stage Two

building the life you really want

Preparation time is now over! You should now be ready to move on to the second stage in our 'getting a life' strategy. This is divided into four main sections:

Nurturing your body, mind and spirit

Developing a happy and fulfilling personal life

Finding satisfaction at work

Connecting with the wider world

Each section covers an arena where your life is 'played out'. In the first of these you will be looking at how well you are nurturing your own personal development and clarifying your own ideas about what would constitute a dream life for you. In the second section we will be exploring ways to make your personal relationships more fulfilling. In the third, our focus will be on your working life and you will be re-evaluating what you need from work (paid or unpaid), how you may be able to improve relationships with colleagues, and how you can keep stress at bay. And in the fourth section, you will be looking at your role in the wider world and seeing if by improving your own involvement with it and making more of a contribution, you can gain a better quality of life for yourself.

Then there is one final very important step in this stage, which will show you how to maintain the balance in your life that you want and need.

Nurturing your body, mind and spirit

STEP 3

Give yourself a health check

Some of you may have wondered why I didn't include health in my list of 'basics' in Step 2. After all, the song you frequently hear people sing in one form or another is 'All you need is health.'

But, of course, this is another of those myths that are fed into our subconscious minds. The reality is that there are many millions of people living right now in very poor health who are enjoying a very full and happy life. Amongst these are also a considerable number who actually have their ill-health to thank for the fact that they are doing so! This is because it was becoming ill that proved a turning point for them. It was the 'wake-up' call that made them think about the impermanence of their existence and their previous lifestyle. Perhaps it also gave them time to plan a strategy which helped them make some changes. But, of course, given a second chance they would have preferred to have their cake and eat it. They usually wish they hadn't needed that kind of wake-up call and often like to warn others about taking their good health too much for granted.

Are you as fit and healthy as you can be?

If you have been attracted to this book, it is unlikely that you are. Your body and mind are most probably not in the best of shapes. First, you are aware that your life could be better, and living with that awareness inevitably puts a strain on the body. This kind of stress, like any other, ensures that organs and muscles never reach their sell-by date.

Secondly, you have probably been either overly or under busy and have not devoted good-enough time to the routine maintenance of your health. The overly busy can't usually find the time for exercise, health check-ups and healthy eating. The under busy can't find the motivation. (Doesn't boredom breed apathy and depression?)

You may not need perfect health to have the life you want. But the more physically and mentally fit you are, the easier it will be to find it. And, needless to say, you might appreciate the extra energy when you start to live it.

The fitter and healthier you are, the easier you will *find* and *keep* the life you really want.

There is an awesome responsibility in 'becoming what we believe ourselves to be'. Yet how infinitely rich our lives become when we can take up that idea – and live by it through every day of our existence.

STEPHANIE DOWRICK

Action time!

- **Check and/or change your exercise routine.** It should be fun and as quickly rewarding as it can be. If you don't enjoy the gym, don't go – even if you have already paid your dues and everyone else appears to be having fun. Try dancing or swimming classes instead, or whatever else appeals.

- **Take de-stressing action before you become stressed.** Release tension from your body by doing a few quick stretches at least every hour.

- **Clear your mind by doing a meditation at least once a day** (see below for a suggestion). If you don't believe it works or that it's just for New Age freaks, beg, borrow or buy a copy of Christina Feldman's *Thorsons Way of Meditation* before the week is out!

A Simple Daily Meditation

– Release the tension out of any taut muscles by tightening and releasing them a few times. Screw up your face and then relax it several times if you have enough privacy to be able to do so.

- Lie or sit in a well-supported position (unless you are well practised in taking up the traditional yoga lotus position that many Eastern practitioners use).
- Close your eyes if you are somewhere where you can.
- Focus your whole awareness on your breathing. Visualize and feel it as it enters and leaves your body. Continue doing this for a minute or so.
- While still following your breathing, now centre your attention on either your heart or at a point inside your head in the direct line of the central point between your eyes. (The latter point is the location of the centre in your brain which controls your 'fight or flight' response.)
- In time to your breathing, start saying in your mind a 'mantra'. This is a word or short phase of your choosing. (For example, 'calm'; 'at peace', or 'I am being'.) Keep repeating your mantra for as long a time as you can spare. When a thought enters your mind, gently refocus your attention on the meditation point you have chosen and continue saying your mantra in time to your breathing.

- **Cut down immediately on your intake of stimulants.** Yes, this is the same old reminder about caffeine, alcohol and cigarettes, and so forth! Magazines, newspapers and TV programmes are always reminding us about how they depress our system and harm our health in the long-term. Most of us know by now that there are much more effective ways to get an energy boost. But do you practise what you hear being preached so often? If not, experiment and experiment until you teach your palate to crave for the good-for-you drinks and snacks. (I was determined to teach myself to like camomile tea which I knew was calming and good for digestion – it took a month or so. Now I can't go to bed without it and I always take some bags with me when I travel. I did the same with porridge and now I start the day with it, even in the summer in southern Spain!)

- **Aim for *quality* sleep, not just the proverbial quantity of eight hours.** Before going to bed:

– de-stress your body with a warm bath and an all-over self-massage with lotion scented with lavender or one of your own favourite oils
– ensure that your mind is fed with peaceful and

positive images (late-night news broadcasts and action thrillers are best avoided)

- stick carefully to a nightly routine (for example, do your going-to-bed chores in the same order / have the same kind of drink at the same time)
- ensure your bedroom is:
  - well-aired (a good supply of oxygen is necessary for body-repair work)
  - looking calm, cosy and tidy (your brain will make you work hard in your dreams if it senses disorder and emotional unrest)
  - quiet (wear earplugs or put the snorers in another room – as indeed I do!)
  - dark (this makes the hormone melatonin kick in which starts off the sleep cycle)

- **Put regular health checks into your diary** – most dentists remind us but does your doctor, osteopath, physiotherapist or any of the others that tend to your body or mind?

- **Clear your kitchen of bad temptation** – fill it with the healthy kind as soon as possible. A costly clean-up of the contents of your cupboards and fridge could be a good test of your commitment to this strategy. Have the courage to waste some bad food instead of your life!

STEP 4

Indulge in self-discovery

This is perhaps the quickest way to make your life more interesting.

Sounds boring or self-indulgent?

If so, your subconscious is probably up to its sabotage tricks again. Whose voices are you hearing? And do you really believe them? Often the sceptics misunderstand what self-discovery is. They can confuse it with self-reflection or self-obsession. It is more than the former and certainly not the latter.

If someone is actively discovering the depths of their personality and potential, I don't believe they could be bored (or boring). Our complex and unique selves are forever changing so we can always surprise ourselves (and therapists like me who may be the witness!).

This positive process is such a crucial part of finding and keeping a meaningful life that I would go as far as to say that it is the sceptics who are 'crazy' to label it self-indulgent. Invariably, people who are at ease with themselves and their world are better at making other people's lives more meaningful than those who are not.

We need to discover and keep on discovering:

Who we are: so we can play to our strengths, alter or manage our weaknesses, and develop the parts of us we want to enhance. (Otherwise we will be the kind of person others thought we were or want us to be, or stay exactly the same as we have always been.)

What we believe in: so we can act with passion and maintain self-respect by living in harmony with our principles.

(Otherwise we will be drawn haphazardly along by the values of other people and a need to earn respect from them.)

What we want: so we can be inspired by our own personal life-dream. (Otherwise we are putty in the hands of fate and others' wants.)

Discovering the depths of your personality and potential is one of the quickest ways to make your life more satisfying and meaningful.

I always wanted to be someone, but I should have been more specific.

LILY TOMLIN

Action time!

- **Set aside at least one evening (but preferably an afternoon) for self-reflection. Make a list of your 10 key strengths** (include a mixture of character, aptitude and skill). Beside each write a statement of intention. This should indicate how you will use each strength to change your life. (For example, *'I will use my compassion to find new friends and add a greater sense of purpose to my life'* / *'I will use my organizational skills to restructure my personal life and plan a new adventure.'*)

- **List six weaknesses and state how you intend to manage or alter them.** (For example, *'The moment I start thinking negatively, I will dip into a book of positive quotations'* (see the *Further Help* section at the end of the book for a recommendation) / *'I will become tidier by getting up 15 minutes earlier and doing some clearing up to music while I am waking up.'*)

- **List three areas of yourself you wish to start developing immediately.** Write a promise for each in relation to improving your life. (For example, *'I will read a book on assertiveness skills so I* *can say "No" more convincingly' / 'I will sign up for an evening class in astronomy to regenerate my curiosity.')*

- **Imagine you are now 80 years old and someone is giving a speech about you and your wonderful personal qualities. Which six qualities would you be proud to hear them praise you for?** (Yes, it could happen!) Beside each write what you need to do in order to live more in harmony with each NOW. (For example, **honesty** – *'I need to be more honest about the fact that I am not enjoying ___ and I am not able to ___'* / **caring for others** – *'I need to commit more time to be with the children and my father.'*)

- **Fill in the gaps in this prophetic story.** (*Note*: this is a story *not* a fairytale!)

In 10 years' time, I will be living in ___with ___. I will enjoy spending most weekends doing ___. I will feel proud to have achieved ___. I will be planning to ___ so that in 20 years' time I will be able to ___.

My life-dream will be realized because by next week I will have started ___, and in six months I will have finished ___ and started ___.

You don't have to suffer continual chaos in order to grow.

LILY TOMLIN

STEP 5

Increase your sensory pleasures

Now *this* step is closer to self-indulgence – and why not?!

Until quite recently, I ran regular personal development groups. We always started each session by sharing something that had given us pleasure either that day or since we last met. Unless they were well-trained regulars, most people found this an excruciatingly difficult exercise. This was not because they were shy (and no, we were not expected to reveal our love-life!). It was because they either hadn't noticed the pleasures they had encountered or they were living a life without them. They were often even more dismayed to find that they couldn't remember what used to give them joy.

Are you heading in that unhappy direction but don't yet know it?! Do you spend so much of your time in your head or giving yourself so much pain that you have almost forgotten what it feels like to feel joy, delight and even passion?

Feeling pleasure *frequently* is a 'must' for anyone who truly wants a quality life. Not only is joy a great end in itself to aim for, it is also the finest fuel of motivation. Kicking and nagging yourself on to a better life certainly won't work. I've seen too many people try this method and fail. An abundance of treats and rewards are what you need.

Give yourself full permission to indulge yourself in more of whatever lights up your sensual fire!

But don't overdose on sensory pleasures – or you'll hear those subconscious string-pullers saying 'I told you so!' You can have too much of this good thing. Living sensually in the present is so pleasurable that it is easy to forget that there is work to be done for your future. So give yourself small measured doses until you are sure that you can handle it! To realize your dreams you need your head and a lot of hard graft as well! Once again it is all about balance, and personally measured balance at that. Some of us are undoubtedly more needy of sensual pleasure than others, but don't we all need (and deserve) enough?

With an eye made quiet by harmony and the deep power of joy, we see into the heart of things.

WILLIAM WORDSWORTH

Action time!

- **Stop reading this book *now* and give your senses a mini-treat.** (If you are in a crowded public place, take care! You may have to use the considerable power of your imagination or wait until you have more privacy.)

  While determinedly ignoring anything which grates against your senses:

  - feast your eyes on the abundance of colours and shapes you see
  - appreciate the beauty and balance of the design around you, both natural and man-made
  - feel as many textures as you can and note the ones that give you pleasure
  - be aware of what you are smelling. Find a scent that is pleasurable and enjoy it
  - listen to the sounds that are around you. Can you find a rhythm or tone that is pleasurable? If not, create one. (Even tone-deaf people can clap and tap!)
  - find something to taste that you know you will enjoy. Savour the flavour for much longer than you normally do.

- **Ask yourself when did you last feel deeply passionate in a positive way** – about a person, a thing, a place or an event? How often do you respond to the world and what is happening with spontaneous joy? Note down two things you can start doing to bring more joy and passion into your *everyday* life? (For example, listen to __ music / watch more comedy programmes / light candles every evening and ...!)

- **Plan at least one knock-out treat for your senses within the next month.** (Don't forget that saying 'The best things in life are free.' Whoever said it first must have had a sensual pleasure in mind!)

STEP 6

Stimulate your creativity

Think about the last time that you saw a group of young toddlers at play. I am sure they must have been absorbed in creating something. Can you remember how much joy and pleasure they were getting from their creations? No one has to compel a toddler to make something out of 'nothing'. They don't need to be shown how to build castles with tins of beans. They do it because they *want* to do it.

And, moreover, while they are absorbed in their creative task these toddlers are not at all bothered about what others are doing. They are not caring about whether anyone else is building a bigger or better sandcastle or more impressive drawing on mum's wall.

But how soon most of these children will lose touch with this natural, enjoyable urge to create!

I have found that rediscovering the potential joy of creativity seems to be one of the important keys to making life more meaningful. But I am not just referring to the kind we associate with art activities. It is possible to be creative in almost every other area of activity as well. Any task that can give us an opportunity to use our natural inventiveness and ingenuity to give birth to something new (whether this is an idea or a material product) has the potential to be creative.

How easy it is to forget this truth. Commonly, most people's everyday work feels very distanced from the end-product they are helping to produce. At home we may feel similarly distanced from products we use, wear and eat. Many years ago I used to love whiling away weekends cooking and making my own and my children's clothes, or making curtains and cushions to decorate our house. Nowadays, many a weekend is 'rushed away' in a stressful trail around supermarkets and shopping malls to buy things made by machines. Then on my return home I may have to persuade myself

I can spare ten minutes to make a fresh stir-fry instead of putting an instant meal in the microwave.

Is your life too full of 'ready-mades'? Would you love to have more opportunity to be more creative? Here are some suggestions and exercises to help you on your way.

Feel the joy and satisfaction of creating something innovative and unique.

If you always do what you've always done, you'll always get what you've always got.

ANON

Action time!

- **Give some time to thinking about the kind of creativity that comes most naturally to you** – thinking back to your toddler days (or the nearest year your memory will allow!) might help. What kind of creation did you enjoy making? For example, did you like building or drawing or making plays or experimenting with working models? If you can't remember, ask someone else who might be able to. You may even have some pictures which would give you a clue.

  Then ask yourself if you could find a way to use this innate part of your personal make-up more in your current life.

- **Use creative people for inspiration** – note down examples of the kind of creative activity that others engage in around you which you admire most. Is it contemporary art, new folk tunes, originally decorated rooms or inventive ways to store their tools? Or is it more to do with people's performance such as new strategies to win games or play brilliantly with the guitar?

- **Once you have given yourself time to mull this thought over, make contact with some of these people and 'pick their brains'.** Ask them how they go about their tasks, how they first became interested and involved, and what they feel when they are doing it. Even if you don't get an idea of where you might start yourself, just talking to them is likely to be inspiring.

- **Find a new creative pastime or course** – use the library or internet to find clubs, societies and courses. Contact professional people (and their organizations) who are involved in creative activities for advice. (I often give advice to people who want to become amateur counsellors so I know that approach can work!) You may need to experiment with a variety of creative activities until you find the one that feels like fun and that is hard to say 'No' to.

- **List some simple ways of using your creativity more in your everyday life** – think of some activities that you could regularly do without having to spend too much money, time, travel or energy on. For example, experiment with a different flower arrangement every two weeks (if you can't buy them around the corner, have a small bunch delivered regularly); invent one recipe a week; add a hand-drawn decoration to your shopping list; rearrange the furniture in one room every month; change your hairstyle or make-up; make and change your own screen saver; use stories to illustrate the point you want to get across in reports or emails or presentations; redesign a border bed for the garden.

- **Check whether any of the so-called creative tasks** (such as painting, drama or playing music) **that you already do are still giving you a 'buzz'**. It is unlikely that they are working well for you (otherwise you would not be reading this book!).

  Maybe these hobbies or jobs have become mundane and no longer feel like an unpredictable adventure. Or perhaps you are trying to do them too perfectly and you need to 'lighten up' when doing them. Maybe, on the other hand, you have changed and the new you simply needs a different creative challenge. (The 25-year-old Gael would have laughed to hear that I am considering writing a novel!)

STEP 7

Nurture your spirit

Maybe it is a sign that I am more of a product of our secular times than I thought that I have chosen to put this step at the end of this section. I would have to agree that finding satisfying ways to nurture my spirit after giving up my religion at the end of my teens was not easy. But, nevertheless, I have never doubted its importance. For many years I did continue to envy those whose faith gave them a clear direction on how to feed their souls. I also worried about having to face a major loss without it, and even used to say I would probably be one of those who begged to be received back into the flock on my deathbed. Maybe I still will, but then again maybe I won't because now, forty years on, I have found many alternative ways to nurture my spirit – and I have survived a nightmare loss.

But what do I mean by 'your spirit'? I know this is a question that some of you may be asking because I hear it posed so often nowadays. In spite of the fact that we are now living in what is frequently described as the Spiritual Age, many people still do not seem to share the same understanding of this word. I have struggled myself to define it and came up with the following personal interpretation.

I think of my spirit as:

- the part of me that has no material form to the human eye
- my unique fundamental nature that came into being the moment I was conceived
- the invisible presence or force that I hope to leave in the world after the death of my body
- my moral and intellectual essence created from my own unique blend of beliefs and values
- the force of my individual energy which is connected to a universal life-force

- the atmosphere or aura that surrounds me which other people sense when they are in my presence.

Although this may not be a water-tight definition, it did help me to clarify what kind of suggestions I could make to help others improve this dimension of their lives. (And certainly being in the business I am in, I know how many people are now seeking this kind of guidance, even if they have a formal religious faith.)

But even if you question my interpretation of spiritual needs, I hope you find that the following suggestions will enrich your life.

Enrich your life with spiritually nurturing and stimulating experiences.

The oceanic feeling of wonder is the common source of religious mysticism, of pure science and art for art's sake; it is their common denominator and emotional bond.

ARTHUR KOESTLER

Action time!

- **After your daily meditation** (remember my suggestion on page 44 – I am sure you have dutifully followed it, haven't you?!) **take a few of these still moments to be aware of your spiritual dimension.** Notice your 'aliveness' and non-physical presence. Be aware of the energy around your body and visualize it meeting and interacting with the other energies in the room.

- **Reflect and list the memorable experiences which you have had in the last year which have either nurtured or helped you feel more connected to your or other people's spirits.** These will obviously vary according to your interpretation of 'spirit', your personality and your life experiences, but they could include:

  – meeting a special person with whom you experienced an instant connection (the soul-mate kind)
  – a moment of deep inner peace on a visit to a beautiful tranquil place such as a rose garden, a church, an exquisitely designed

room, a cave, a mountain peak or a beach at sunset or dawn

- seeing a 'stunning' object of art such as a painting or sculpture or piece of jewellery, or seeing a man-made wonder of the world with which you felt an immediate connection
- a visit to a museum which gave you an 'eerie' sense of contact with the ancient world
- being present at an uplifting live experience of art such as a concert or a dance performance
- reading something such as a moving poem or uplifting story and feeling as though you have connected with some deep truth
- hearing a 'divine' sound such as a choir in a church or the song of a bird or the bells of goats on a mountain
- suddenly breaking into wild and spontaneous laughter or dancing with a group of people
- praying alone in a peaceful setting or with a large group in a public place
- eating or drinking something that looked, smelled and tasted 'sublime'
- having an 'extra-sensory' communication with someone (for example, crossed letters or someone ringing you just after you were thinking about them)

- an intimate, mutually loving experience that brought you into deep contact with someone else's spiritual self
- being present at a significant birth or death
- feeling 'infected' by the warm energy given off by children playing 'make-believe' in a totally believable way
- a shared deep emotional reaction to a joyous or shocking event with a group of people
- feeling the restorative touch of a healing person
- sensing the power of a charismatic person as they entered a room
- sensing the presence of someone you loved who has died
- having the 'transcendental' experience of feeling separated from your body after a meditation or a deeply relaxing experience such as a massage or being bathed in warm sunshine
- watching a candle flicker in the dark and experiencing a subsequent feeling of lightness and peace.

- **Recall a few (don't depress yourself with too many!) examples of the opposite kind of experiences which you had during the last year** (i.e. those which you feel were damaging to your spirit or made you feel cut off from that part of yourself, perhaps for a prolonged period).

- **Reflect on whether you had an adequate supply of spiritually nurturing and stimulating experiences last year.** If you would like to build more into your life, make a note of what kind you need and how you can arrange for this to happen. (For example, make time to be with certain people / visit more gardens and galleries / learn meditation / go to church more often, and so forth.) Strengthen your resolve by telling someone of your intention or making a concrete date or plan for doing them.

How beautiful it is to do nothing, and rest afterward.

SPANISH PROVERB

Developing a happy and fulfilling personal life

Lots of people want to ride with you in the limo, but what you want is someone who will take the bus with you when the limo breaks down.

OPRAH WINFREY

STEP 8

Deepen your key intimate relationships

Sorry, this step is not about sex! (But there are plenty of other books on that subject!) It is instead about 'unconditional love' (or, in simple terms, 'Love without strings'). It is about deepening those relationships with people who could, or already do, value, respect and stand by you *in spite* of the fact that you might be:

spotty; larger than size 10; the owner of a raucous laugh; prone to the odd temper tantrum; untidy; bossy; hopeless at scoring goals; poorer, richer, more beautiful or more talented than them!

When we are with people who love us in this way, we should feel safe and understood and totally free to be ourselves. We should feel we can 'tell them anything' and, even though they may occasionally be shocked or disapprove of our behaviour or disagree with our viewpoint, we 'know' that they won't withdraw their love. You may find that your communication in these relationships is imbued with extra-sensory characteristics. (They are your 'soul-mates'.) Often people say they can 'sense' what the other is feeling and anticipate what is going to be said without having to be told.

How many of these kinds of intimate relationships do we need?

This is an impossible question to answer with any surety. Emotional needs and the quality of feelings cannot be measured. But, nevertheless, it is a question which in my experience is repeatedly asked by people who are trying to 'get a life', so I will attempt an answer.

I believe that in order to maintain a life of quality most of us need to be able, when 'our chips are down', to count on **three to six adult–adult relationships where unconditional mutual love is flourishing.** If we have children and/or we have a large extended loving family we may obviously have much more. But what is probably important to remember is that in the intimacy business, **it's quality not quantity that counts.**

But perhaps you are thinking, *'Help! I don't have even this small number of intimate relationships.'*

That's no problem as long as you ignore some of the unhelpful myths that surround this kind of love. The most common one is that 'the best kind of love' (i.e. unconditional love) is always delivered and taken away randomly by the hand of fate. (Cupid descends and smites us or he doesn't / you can 'fall-out' of love without your consent / Earth mothers and loving children are 'born' not bred!) The truth is that this kind of love, like any other, can and *is* more frequently developed as a relationship deepens.

The second most common myth that might have been sabotaging your relationship potential is that such love is best derived from our relatives (as the 'blood is thicker than water' stories warn us!) or our life-partner (as the Hollywood movies suggest). The stark reality of the modern world is that our families are so scattered, scarred and often 'broken' that many people are barely known, let alone loved in any shape or form by their relatives, and some rarely see their spouses.

Of course, the place where most people first experienced and learned naturally about the give and take of this kind of love was in their childhood family home. Some of us however were not so lucky and, as a result, we don't have high expectations of love. (*'Just my luck – she was a two-timer' / 'You can't count on anybody but yourself in the end'.*) We also have to learn what it looks like (*'Is this true love?' Do you* really *love me?'*) and learn the skills to manage it (*'I always make a mess of deep relationships'*).

If you are in this position, don't ever believe that the quality of relationships that you consciously choose to deepen is of an inferior sort. The unconditional love that is grown in relationships of our own adult choosing can be just as precious and enriching as any that may land on our genetic doorstep or any that may set fire to our sexual chemistry.

Below are some suggestions for checking out and deepening the intimacy potential of your relationships. But be careful not to set yourself up for disappointment – don't forget that you will never be able to achieve unconditional love from *any* human 100% of the time.

Tips for Deepening Intimacy

- **Protect quality time alone together.** Make sure that you can sometimes be together or talk together on the phone without being interrupted or too distracted.

- **Share feelings and thoughts openly about 90% of the time.** But also show respect for each others' right to hold back sometimes. Don't be seduced by the myth that 'best friends' and 'happy couples' have to tell each other *everything*.

- **Pick up on the non-verbal language and check that you are reading it right.** But don't claim to be their mind reader, however well you know them. (For example, say *'Your face seemed to adopt a harassed-looking expression when you were talking about our holiday to Julian. Is that what you really feel about it?'* rather than, *'So that's what you really felt about our holiday is it – no,* *don't try and pretend to me that you enjoyed it. I know what you are thinking.')*

- **Initiate regular joint relationship spot-checks.** There is no need for this to be a 'heavy time'. Kick it off with some simple self-disclosure and then a question. (For example, *'I keep thinking how lucky I am to have a friend like you, but I wonder if I am being a good-enough friend to you?'* or *'I'm feeling a bit frustrated because we've only managed to speak to each other once this week. What do you feel?')*

- **Confront problems in their early infancy, but do so at the right time and in the right place.** Frustration and disappointment don't have to be given an *instant* airing – only a 'soon-enough' one. (For example, if someone is obviously tired and stressed wait until they are less so. If they don't show signs of making a quick enough recovery from their state, at least give them some warning that you want 'a talk' and agree a time.)

- **Suggest more silent and separate times together.** The deeper the relationship, the more *comfortable* you should feel in the company of each other when nothing appears to be happening between you. (For example, you are not talking and each is engaged in their individual thoughts or activities.) But be careful. These kind of silent bonding times will deepen a good relationship, but can have the very opposite effect on one that is not going well.

– **Keep having fun together**, even if you do not have time to do much else together for a while. Even the most unconditional of all loves will wilt under the onslaught of continuous 'heavy weather'.

My commitment to my people, to the millions of South Africans I would never know or meet, was at the expense of the people I knew best and loved most.

To be a father of a nation is a great honour and joy, but to be a father of a family is a greater joy. But it was a joy I had far too little of.

NELSON MANDELA

Action time!

- **Reflect on your childhood experience of intimacy and unconditional love.** Were you left with an emotional hole? If so, vow to take *extra* care of your most intimate relationships. For the rest of your life you could, for example, be either unconsciously driven to overfill that love-hole or protect yourself from the hurting potential of intimacy. Explore ways to heal (as best as any of us ever can) your childhood hurts. For example:

  - Spend an afternoon browsing in the self-help section of a good bookshop until you find some books about relationships that may be able to help you. (I have recommended one or two in the *Further help* section at the end of the book.)
  - Attend workshops on this subject. (See *Further help* for details of useful websites.)
  - Have some counselling or therapy sessions.
  - Find alternatives to the relationships you missed out on. (For example, let yourself be spoiled by the office 'mother hen'; make friends with older neighbours and get yourself

some honorary grandparenting; cultivate one of your friends to be more like a sister or a brother by inviting them to your family 'dos'.)

- **Check the intimacy potential of your current relationships:**

- Make a list of the 12 key relationships with adults you currently have in your life. (This could be family, lovers or close friends.)
- Make a list of six of your worst faults. (That's an easy one to answer for a change, isn't it?!)
- Ask yourself who amongst these 12 people know about these faults. If they do know or were to find out, how do (or might) they react to them?
- Are they demanding (or would they demand) that you change them?
- Do you think that they will (or would) continue to love you even if you did not change them?
- Imagine yourself in a crisis situation (helpless in hospital or even guilty in prison!). You are in dire need of emotional support (rather than practical help or guidance). Which three of these people would you most like to have by your side?

- **Improve the quality of your key relationships:**
  - Give the current state of each of the three relationships that you selected above a rough rating against each of these six aspects (1 = excellent; 10 = poor and 5 = the pass rate!):

    1. amount of quality time spent together
    2. level of open sharing
    3. tolerance of each other's differences
    4. level of trust in confidentiality
    5. level of trust in loyalty
    6. long-term prospects

  - Use the tips on pages 83–5 to help you reflect on initiatives *you* can take to improve the lower ratings (for example, to be more open and frank yourself / commit more time to the relationship / stop criticizing / suggest plans for dates far into the future / read books on gender issues / attend workshops or counselling together).

- **Let yourself off the 'intimacy hook' when you need to** – you could have a good reason for not wanting to be too close to someone or anyone for a while. (Perhaps you are still recovering from a severe loss or hurt or you need time to yourself to think.)

- **Tell people clearly you want to stay in 'shut-down' mode for a while** – don't wait for them to feel hurt or rejected or frustrated. (Many close relationships are improved by some periods of mutually agreed 'breathers'. You have a right to ask for space sometimes.)

- **Find a temporary channel for your loving nature** – for example, get a pet (my dog Basil loves me even when I short-change him on the walk front, and he knows when I am sad even when I am pretending to be happy!) or give some time to a charity for deprived children or disabled adults.

- **Move on to the next step and divert your energy into improving your social life.**

No one has ever loved anyone the way they want to be loved.

MIGNON McLAUGHLIN

STEP 9

Update your social life

While finding happy, fulfilling, intimate relationships is for the majority of people the most important aspect of their personal life, it is rarely enough. Most of us want and need additional relationships of a less intense nature as well. We want to be able to spend some of our personal time with a much wider range of people and have some activities that our nearest and dearest might run a mile from. (My husband falls asleep in some of the plays I choose to go to and I find some of the music he likes an irritating cacophony!)

A good social life not only provides us with extra fun and stimulation, it also can be a great source of support in times of difficulty. It can simply provide us with diversion and perspective by giving us an

People change and forget to tell each other.

LILLIAN HELLMAN

absorbing activity to 'get lost in'. Or it may provide us with very practical help from acquaintances who do not need (or particularly want to become involved in) the emotional quagmires of our more intimate life. (For example, the friendly face from the gym who spontaneously offers transport when they hear you receive a call asking you to collect your sick child from school, or a fellow dance class student who takes you for a 'no-strings attached' drink because you look as though you need cheering up after a particularly hard day.)

A good social life not only provides us with extra fun and stimulation, it can also be a great source of support in times of difficulty.

In the old days (pick your era!) many people developed a very satisfactory social life centred around their church or their place of work. Now more and more of us no longer attach ourselves to a specific religious centre, and at the same time we are finding that our jobs are presenting fewer and fewer opportunities to make social contacts. The CEO's may still be able to 'buddy up' on golf courses, but pressure on time and budgets and the change to flexi-time and home and mobile working is fast killing off the kind of sports and social events that used to bond together most other workers.

But let's not forget a social diary overflowing with contacts and activities is not necessarily a good enough one either. I know many people with these who are quite obviously wasting away hours of their lives in the company of people who do not stimulate them and would probably never support them or are engaging in activities which they no longer enjoy.

Few of us give the same amount of thought and consideration to *choosing* and *proactively procuring* a satisfying social life as we do when we are mapping out a working life for ourselves. You may have collected your network of friends and acquaintances over many years in a haphazard way and you may be coasting along doing pastimes and sports simply because they are the ones you have always done. You may not have even stopped to consider whether your social life has gone past its sell-by date. But, equally, you could have been 'moaning' about it for years but been too fearful or pressurized to set about 'shedding the old to make way for

The only way to have a friend is to be one.

RALPH WALDO EMERSON

the new'. Either way, a spot-check in this area will do no harm. A great social life may never be able to offer you many deep and meaningful experiences, but what the hell! Who wants these 100% of the time anyway?

If you want people to be glad to meet you, you must be glad to meet them – and show it.

GOETHE

Action time!

- **Here are some examples of the personal needs that are commonly met from a good social life.** Feel very free to alter and leave out the ones that are irrelevant to you. Add some other more specific ones that you know you have. Write each one at the head of a separate sheet of paper:

  - **fun** (spontaneous letting your hair down and having a laugh)
  - **support** (the 'no-questions-asked' kind)
  - **sports indulgence** (the active and armchair varieties)
  - **physical care** (from exotic health spas to yoga in the school hall)
  - **intellectual stimulation** (stretching your mind and keeping it agile)
  - **creative stimulation** (encourages you to make and innovate)
  - **moral guardianship** (challenges to your principles and prejudices)
  - **spiritual nurture** (escapes from the material world)
  - **adventure** (the curiosity and adrenaline stimulators)

- **comfort zoning** (escapes to safety and predictability)
- **devilment** (from pure gossip to the unprintable!)

- **Draw a line down the centre of the page.** On one side enter the names of friends or groups of acquaintances that help you to fulfil this need. On the other side add any activities that you do which help you to meet this need.

- **Reflecting on each page in turn, ask yourself the following questions:**

  - how well is this need met by my current social life? (You could give it a rating using a scale of 1–10.)
  - do I need to find new people to help me meet this need?
  - do I need to alter or extend my relationships with anyone to help me meet this need better?
  - do I need to look for additional activities to meet these needs?

- **Use the back of each page to note down actions you might want to take to ensure that**

your social needs are better catered for. (For example, joining a dance club / taking up a new sport / joining a friendship network / taking lunch in a café instead of at home, and so forth.)

STEP 10

Make your home a more relaxing place to be in

Do you often hear yourself apologizing for the state of your home when visitors drop in on you?

Do you find you often lose things amidst the clutter?

Are you often running out of supplies such as loo rolls, sugar or flour because you have forgotten to buy them?

If you don't, feel free to skip this section and move on.

But I am fairly certain that many readers of this book will recognize these classic symptoms. In my experience, they are very common amongst people who feel they are not in control of their lives.

Our home should be a place that nurtures us. When we are in it we should be able to feel relaxed enough to recharge our batteries and have fun with the people we love. A home that looks untidy or has more hidden depths of disorder is not one that can support a life of quality. It drains our energy with unnecessary shame, guilt and stress.

An early adult life-crisis forced this message home to me. Some heavy confrontation from a therapist and subsequent soul-searching helped me to change my disorderly habits that I once thought were intrinsic to my 'interesting' personality. Worse still, I confess that previously I thought the clutter enhanced my attractiveness to people who shared my bohemian style of life. My prejudices led me to believe that concerns about domestic duties were the province of people who hadn't anything better to do with their lives.

How wrong I was! Not only have I proved this for myself, I have now seen hundreds and hundreds of clients learn this life lesson as well. I cannot recall having worked with a single person on 'getting a life' who has not at some stage done a major revamp of their home-life and benefited enormously from doing so.

Although home organization still doesn't come that easily for me, it will always now have high priority. When I see the first signs of disorder setting in, I remind myself I have many better things to do with my life than clearing up avoidable messes. Then I throw myself into a major sort-out mode before the 'clutter' can sabotage the life I value.

The following suggestions are the result of observing what has helped most people in similar situations. But they may not be exactly the kind your home-life needs. If on reading through them they are not, you may be advised to get some more specialist help in this area. A visit to a bookshop or library to look at books on home management might be a useful starting point.

Our home should be a place that nurtures us, where we can recharge our batteries and have fun with the people we love.

The most instructive experiences are those of everyday life.

FRIEDRICH NIETZSCHE

Action time!

- **Set aside one half a day in your diary for a radical home clearout.** Set aside another half day a week or so later for **a major reorganization.** Limit yourself to only half a day because any more time usually proves to be too exhausting and depressing to be useful.

- **Tell someone about your plan and invite them to inspect or check up on the result.**

- **Before the day of your clearout organize the following:**

– a stock of food and drinks for treats (enough for *many* breaks)
– your favourite music (but make sure it is energizing rather than relaxing!)
– at least four different coloured or numbered bags and boxes. For example:

1. rubbish
2. charity
3. for sale/presents
4. filing/storage

– a reward (ready to have on the same day – over-delayed gratification is not motivating enough!).

- **Write out (and pin up) some *unbreakable* rules to beat your hoarding habits.** (For example, dispose of anything not worn or used for two years; pass on books never likely to be read or opened again; no re-reading of old magazines; bin everything in pending tray dated over a month ago.)

- **On your day of action, switch all phones to their answering service and start doing exactly what a good burglar would do, i.e. turn out and over *every* 'nook and cranny'.** Have a short recovery break before ruthlessly sorting everything into your labelled containers.

- **Before your organizational half-day, ensure that you have bought the means to be able to subdivide and label and file all your drawers, shelves (including those for books and CDs), cupboards and hanging rails.** Your aim will be to make the contents of all of these easily visible and readily accessible. To help you to do this there are now many different firms specializing in home storage solutions, but cheaper alternatives such as old shoeboxes and rolls of clear polythene bags and labels should be quite sufficient.

- **Make a list of all your major household tasks** (for example, shopping / washing / cleaning, and so forth). Over the next two weeks, collect as many tips and information on helpful services as you can about doing these chores (for example, ask organized friends and colleagues); read relevant books (see the *Further help* section for suggestions); email for advice to household magazines; research e. commerce solutions (see *Further help* for possible web solutions).

- **If you share your home, call a family or house-mates' meeting to allocate tasks and agree rotas.** (It is a myth that happy households don't need these. You have probably noticed already that Love does not magically transform some people into tidy orderly beings!) Stop your meeting becoming another chance to have a chat or a moan by insisting that it is 'formalized'. Run it in a business-like and speedy manner with deadlines, clear objectives, an agenda, a chairperson and note-taker, votes and follow-up dates. (And remember that there are better times for sorting out any relationship conflicts that may emerge!)

- **Set six-monthly dates in your diary for overviews of household and personal finances.** Book in professional advice if needed – it will probably save you money, but if you haven't enough now, many Citizens Advice centres offer free advice. Resolve never again to wait for the crises.

- **Treat your house to a professional spring clean.** (No money? – ask a friend and then return the favour later. Cleaning up someone else's mess is usually less boring than doing your own.) While your house is being transformed, take yourself to your favourite café or health spa. While you are there, make three new resolutions. (For example, shop only once a week and always take a list; set aside the first Monday evening of each month for a major home-tidy and organization / throw or give away one item of clothing for every new one bought / freeze food before it goes past its sell-by-date and get a window cleaner with the money saved.)

Spend the afternoon. You can't take it with you.

ANNIE DILLARD

Finding satisfaction at work

Men are not free when they are just doing what they like ... men are only free when they are doing what their *deepest self* likes. And there is getting down to the deepest self. It takes some diving.

D. H. LAWRENCE

STEP 11

Ensure your work is meeting your psychological needs

Work that satisfies a good proportion of our psychological needs is the kind of work that doesn't *feel* like work. It is the sort that doesn't take a motivational 'carrot' or a punishment 'stick' from anyone else to make us do it. We labour at it because we feel inwardly driven and are inwardly satisfied. We may sometimes refer to it as our 'vocation' or our 'calling' or our 'mission in life'.

But, of course, the kind of dream work that turns you on could feel like pure hell to someone else! This is because we all have our own individual and sometimes quite complex package of psychological needs. However, there are two basic ones that I have found most people who are unhappy with their working life seem to benefit from examining.

So let's begin by looking at these.

The first of these is **the need to be needed**. For a job to be satisfying, we must *at the very least* feel that what we are doing is worthwhile. Even if we are the tiniest cog in a gigantic global production wheel, we must *know* that our contribution counts. We must believe that the end-result of our effort will make a difference to someone or something.

If we don't think that we are doing a meaningful job, our mental health (and therefore our quality of life) almost certainly suffers. The moment we stop feeling useful, our self-esteem takes a nose-dive. That's why the empty nest syndrome, redundancy and retirement can spark off depression and self-destructive habits even amongst the wealthy and previously successful.

The other psychological need that must be met to some degree is one that you might not even expect to get satisfied through work. It is **the need to be happy.** You wouldn't be unusual if you regarded your job as an 'unfortunate necessity' or purely a means to the end where you think you will find happiness.

Perhaps your dream is that one day you will win or earn enough money to enable you to stop working forever. If so, it may be helpful to remind yourself that it is possible to have the very opposite dream. Even hidden amongst the crowds queuing up for lottery tickets each week, there are many people whose work both feeds their self-esteem *and* gives them joy and contentment. These are the ones who will *choose* to go on working for as long as they possibly can – however much they win. (And no, they are not 'workaholics'. They should not be confused with those who are neurotically compelled to over work.)

I must now declare my own cards. I am one of those people who find their work so satisfying that they continually invite too much of it into their life! I am often openly envied and told I am so 'lucky' to be in that position. But I know that (however arrogant this may sound) 'luck' has played a *very* minor role in making this happen. Like the vast majority of people whom I have met who also love and respect their work, at a certain point in my life I refused to settle for anything less. From a very early age, I have consciously put job satisfaction as one of my top priorities. Even when I was seriously poor, I rarely felt even tempted to take the less self-rewarding job because it paid more, had more prestige or was conveniently situated. I cannot adequately explain why I adopted this particular value. I certainly am no saint and I cannot recall any role-models guiding me in that direction. Perhaps two or three bites at 'deadly' or stressful jobs and a few more interesting work tasters early in my career may have convinced me.

But your life experience and personality may well have led you to adopt different priorities. You certainly don't have to love your job as much as I love mine in order to achieve a life of quality. You may choose a less fulfilling but more financially rewarding one so that you can have a more luxurious personal life. If that is your choice, you could use some of these exercises (and the next two steps of this strategy) as a way of checking that at least a certain proportion of the tasks that you do are enjoyable and meaningful. Alternatively, it may help you to identify some opportunity for voluntary work which will fulfil your psychological needs.

Paid or unpaid work can be one of the most rewarding and enjoyable ways to satisfy a high proportion of our psychological needs.

A musician must make music, an artist must paint, a poet must write, if he is to be ultimately at peace with himself.

ABRAHAM MASLOW

Action time!

- **Look at the list of psychological needs which are commonly met through work on the opposite page and note down the 10 most important ones for you.** Reflect on how well your current job (and/or some of the specific tasks within it) is meeting these needs. Once again, you could use a scale of 1–10 to rate them.

Examples of Psychological Needs

Use this list to stimulate your thinking around your own key psychological needs that you are looking for your work to fulfil. You will notice that some of these words are more or less interchangeable. So, when choosing your list, bear this in mind. Aim to include the widest variety of needs as is possible. It would be a pointless task to choose 10 synonyms, but if when looking through the list you do find yourself attracted to the same kind of need, take notice. This is useful information for you to take on board.

self-esteem	peace of mind	closeness
recognition	privacy	inclusion
appreciation	independence	sociability
challenge	autonomy	altruism
achievement	flexibility	learning
competition	reassurance	curiosity
power	dependency	stimulation
responsibility	support	excitement
status	trust	creation
control	security	innovation
influence	affiliation	
acquisition	affection	

- **Think about what you might need to do in order to get more of these needs met in your current work.** For example:

  responsibility – ask for promotion
  adventure – seek more interesting or high-profile or cutting-edge projects
  esteem – say a firm 'No' to extra tasks which prevent you from being successful at your core business
  affection – give more compliments to colleagues and be more polite and attentive to customers.

- **If you have 'drawn a blank' on the last exercise, plan some serious job-hunting or work rescheduling before accepting your 'fate' to work in such an unsatisfying way.** (For example, make a date with a careers advice professional / read *What Colour Is Your Parachute?* (see *Further help* for details) / register with a recruitment agency / discuss early retirement options with the Human Resources department / regularly download information from relevant web sites (see the *Further help* section) on how to gain better work/life balance / research other possible working arrangements that are fast becoming more available, such as flexi-time, part-time, job-sharing, regular employment breaks, work periods at home, annual hours (to be done whenever and wherever) or consider self-employment.

- **Write down the fears that might stop you from making the changes you need to make in order to get more of these needs met.** Beside each, note an action you could take which will help you control this fear. (Please note that to aim for control as opposed to elimination is more than good enough.

A manageable degree of fear or anxiety helps motivate us.)

For example:

- **fear of failure:** remind yourself what you have learnt from mistakes you have made in the past / make a contingency plan / keep contact with friends who are optimistic and boost your self-esteem.
- **fear of losing money:** re-read your notes from Step 2 and review your basic needs provision / seek financial advice from a professional / get some perspective by holidaying in places where people live happily on much lower incomes than you currently have.
- **fear of not being liked:** remind yourself of your right to be assertive, different and happy / spend more time with people who respect these rights / practise making new friends now
- **fear of being taken advantage of:** read up on assertiveness and anger management strategies.

STEP 12

Make your work pressures work for you

Many of you reading this book are highly likely to be working under great pressure, even if you love your job. But it is important to remember that, contrary to much scaremongering in the press, stress is not an inevitable outcome of working under pressure. Indeed, pressure, when it is well managed, can have the very opposite effect. It can be a positive force to help you find success and psychological satisfaction at work.

The initial chemical effects on our bodies when we are under pressure have the potential to be both physically energizing and psychologically motivating. If we are in a positive frame of mind, we will experience the physiological changes that the surge of increased adrenaline produces as a feeling of excitement. In this emotional state we will have a heightened awareness of the opportunities before us and our minds will think more quickly and creatively about strategies and solutions.

If, on the other hand, we are in a negative state of mind we will experience the same 'butterflies' in our stomach and pounding in our heart as fear. As a result we will only have eyes for problems and obstacles and become panicked. Our minds will freeze or race around in circles with obsessively anxious thoughts. Then we will either become belligerent and stroppy or we will start to run away or lock ourselves defensively in the rut of our comfort zone. (And you cannot get much of a life while fighting, running away or being shackled to one spot!)

Obviously there is a limit to the amount of excitement that any living body can take. When we reach our own personal pressure threshold there is a danger that we can become over-excited and overconfident. But by clarifying some objective criteria to assess pressure levels, and setting aside regular times for relaxation, self-reflection and feedback, it is possible to stay within your 'positive pressure zone'. Not only will you enjoy your work much more while you are there, you should also have the reward of better results.

Pressure, when it is well managed, can be a positive force to help you find success and happiness at work.

The greatest discovery of my generation is that the human being can alter his life by altering his attitudes of mind.

WILLIAM JAMES

Action time!

- **Before setting off for work tomorrow (and every working day hereafter!), make time to do at least 10 minutes of an activity which you enjoy.** (For example, a leisurely read of the lifestyle section of the paper or a chapter of a novel; a soak in the bath to your favourite music, or a potter in the garden de-heading roses.)

- **Make a resolution to do at least 3 short (5–10 minutes) relaxation activities during each working day.** Doing this is far more effective than a longer relaxation at the weekend. (For example, a short meditation before your morning coffee break – see page 44 for a suggestion); some breathing exercises and yoga-style stretches before lunch, or closing your eyes for a few minutes before going into a meeting and in your 'mind's eye' taking yourself to one of your favourite peaceful spots.)

- **Make it a habit to finish each working day with five minutes calm reflection on what you have enjoyed and done well.** (Worrying about tomorrow is not allowed during this time!)

- **Write down three observable things which you tend to do or not do when you are becoming overexcited or are on the verge of becoming stressed.** (For example, rush in late for work or appointments; lose your car keys; talk too fast on the phone or in meetings and others find it difficult to 'get a word in edgeways'; wear the same clothes two days in a row; wear chipped nail polish, and so forth.) Show this list to several colleagues and ask them to let you know the moment they notice you doing any of these things. (They may also be able to suggest other more important examples you hadn't thought of!)

- **Think back to a time in the past when being under pressure produced a positive result,** such as a time when you:

  - were 'pushed to your limits' and as a result actually achieved more than you thought you were capable of. (For example, one of my best books was written in between rushing from one end of England to the other when I had to keep two homes and two businesses ticking over.)
  - had an idea which proved to be very valuable. (For example, one of my best business ideas

arose when my financial back was pushed firmly against the wall by a sudden recession.)

- developed a new or closer friendship as a result of working with someone in pressurized circumstances. (For example, the classic example of this is the closeness that develops amongst soldiers during times of war, but I also know that a similar closeness is forged amongst city workers who are forced to burn the midnight oil when international deals are being negotiated.)

- **Choose one positive scene from these remembered examples which you could regularly recall as a powerful reminder that being under pressure can produce positive results** (for example, the moment you achieved success, had the great idea, or enjoyed a celebration drink with colleagues). This works because the 'chemical factory' in our brain does not make any distinction between a visually imagined situation and a real one.

- **You could 'anchor' this scene more firmly in your brain's emotional memory bank by doing the following exercise:**

Take yourself to a place where you can become deeply relaxed (for example, a warm aromatic bath). Replay your scene over and over again in your mind, making sure that you use as many of your senses as you can to bring the scene alive in your imagination. Visualize the colours and shapes; recall the scents and sounds and textures. Then consciously intensify the image (as though you were seeing it on a giant cinema screen with digital sound) while at the same time making a small movement (for example, touching two fingers together or curling one of your big toes). Repeat the visualization of your scene together with the movement three times.

The next time you begin to feel negative under pressure, take a couple of deep breaths, repeat your small movement and revisualize your scene. Your brain will then automatically switch rapidly over from its negative mode into a more positive one. As a result, you should find yourself feeling excited rather than fearful and will begin to view the situation as a challenge rather than a problem.

STEP 13

'Professionalize' your working relationships

At first glance, I am aware that this may sound strange advice from someone who has spent a good part of their career trying to 'humanize' the workplace. But perhaps asking yourself a few questions may help you to understand what this step is really about.

- Do you ever have difficulty in saying 'No' to people with whom you work – even though not doing so gives you a great deal of stress or stops you from working as well as you could?
- Have you had 'sleepless nights' or other serious anxiety symptoms as a result of making a necessary decision at work which upset or hurt others?
- Do you ever feel that gender differences or sexual attraction gets in the way of developing

the best working relationship with some people?

- Have you sometimes found it difficult to spontaneously share your successes for fear of making certain colleagues (or customers) envious or hurting their self-esteem?
- Do you ever withhold feedback which could be useful for fear of upsetting or embarrassing someone or making them dislike you?
- Have you ever felt more driven to achieve something at work because you wanted to prove something to someone for emotional rather than career reasons?
- Have you ever regretted crying or losing your temper at work because someone that you work with wasn't 'nice' to you?
- Do you ever envy the people who seem to be able to work most of the time without the emotional restrictions that the above can bring?

If you have answered yes to any of the above (however hesitantly!) read on! One reason why you may not be having the life you want is that your strings could be being pulled inappropriately and unnecessarily by colleagues, clients or customers.

There is no way that I am suggesting that we turn the clock back and return to the typical kind of work environments of 20–50 years ago. These were often emotionally sterile places. Feelings were locked away and working relationships were dictated by the role carried out by a person with virtually no regard for the human being within. But perhaps you could become more assertive (rather than passive or aggressive) and take better control of your feelings in certain situations. This way you could still have warm human relationships without the restrictions, risks, worry and time-wasting that operating in a less professional way can bring.

Maintaining professional relationships with colleagues while on the job will help everyone to work well. This can be achieved even by warm, caring people!

To maintain positive power and an ability to set limits successfully, you need a new kind of relationship with your emotions, one where you run them instead of them running you.

MARIA ARAPAKIS

Action time!

- **Make a list of 10 key colleagues, customers and suppliers** (choose your mixture according to the work you do). Reflect on your relationship with each in turn by asking yourself these questions:

  - **What outcome do I need to achieve in my contact with this person?** (For example, an efficiently run office / successful surgery / well-cut hairstyle / four sales contracts per month / balanced accounts / a well-serviced car / stock delivered on time, and so forth.)
  - **How important is it for this person to like me in order to achieve the outcome I need?** (Again you could use a 1–10 rating.) The less important it is to be liked, the less time you need to spend relationship building during work time. (You could still have a more personal relationship out of work if both of you are able to keep your boundaries clear.)
  - **What kind of emotion (and to what degree) does my interaction with this person generally generate?** Note the particular relationships where a high degree of emotion is involved

and what you will do to keep it in control. (For example: *'Whenever I know I am likely to feel irritated, I will take three deep breaths before ringing' / 'Whenever I feel sorry for a person, I will talk the situation over with my boss to check that I have not lost perspective.'*)

- **What degree of 'assertiveness' do I need to use with this person to ensure that the outcome is achieved?** The level of assertiveness you should use should vary appropriately. Imagine a sliding scale of assertiveness with low (almost passive) at one end and high (almost aggressive) the other end. (For example, low might be appropriate to appease an angry customer or authoritarian elderly boss who isn't going to change! High might be appropriate for someone who is quite lazy and takes advantage too easily or someone who is lower in the hierarchy of an emergency services organization. Vow to read a book on assertiveness if you need further clarification. (See the *Further help* section for a recommendation.)

• **Make three resolutions for the next month which will help you to keep certain relationships more on a professional footing.** Add what specific action you could take to ensure this resolution is kept. For example:

Listen but don't counsel when someone shares a personal problem – *'I will listen and indicate empathy but hold back from giving any advice other than where they could go to get more help.'*

Stop business calls becoming chats that I can't break off – *'I will always indicate (or ask for) at the outset of a telephone call what the purpose of the call is and how long it will take.'*

Be more aware of my own personal agendas – *'I will check my motivation each time I say 'Yes' or 'No' to helping someone by asking myself if my response is professionally appropriate or has a hidden personal agenda.')*

- Re-read Steps 8 and 9 and resolve to ensure your intimacy and social needs are adequately met outside your working life.

People who can't say 'No' lose control of their lives, they become victims at the mercy of requests from anyone who decides to ask a favour … the sad thing is that they are not generally much fun to be with as they have sold their character for the need to be liked.

DR BRIAN ROET

[illegible]

People who can't say No lose control of their lives, they become victims at the mercy of requests from anyone who decides to ask a favor . . . the sad thing is that they are not generally much fun to be with as they have sold their character for the need to be liked

[illegible]

Connecting with the wider world

We cannot live only for ourselves.
A thousand fibres connect us with
our fellow men; and among those
fibres, as sympathetic threads, our
actions run as causes, and they
come back to us as effects.

HERMAN MELVILLE

STEP 14

Make a contribution to your community

Much of the strategy covered so far has been centred around getting more of your own needs and wants met. This step is (at its face value anyway) about quite the opposite. It is about evaluating how much you are giving to others with no immediate or obvious reward for you.

It is hard to write on this subject without sounding as though I am standing on 'the moral high ground'. So hard, in fact, that I was sorely tempted to leave it out altogether! But I want to include it because I know that it has been such an important step for so many people I have known who were struggling to find more meaning and satisfaction in their lives.

It has been interesting to observe over the years how through finding a way to give more unselfishly to the wider community, my clients (and me!) have often reaped many rewards for themselves. These have tended to range from inner improvements, such as increased self-esteem and peace of mind, to a more exciting lifestyle with increased adventure and fun. This has occurred not just through the more obvious self-fulfilling projects like Comic Relief (a major UK national fundraising event for deprived children run by famous comedians) and charity bike rides in faraway places, but also through more low-key activities such as picking up litter and helping in local hospitals.

Being unhappy with our lives inclines most ordinary mortals towards egocentricity. Personal problems have a habit of narrowing our interests and our concerns. Perhaps we can blame our basic survival instincts for forcing us into corners to lick our wounds and reserve energy and other resources for our own needs and those of our loved ones. The 'devils' amongst us may not give a second thought to this phenomenon. But most people I know feel guilty and become more depressed when they watch wars and environmental disasters and other communal problems unfold on their TV screens, whilst they know that they are doing very little to help anyone outside their immediate social circle.

So let's assume that *you* are now 'sorted'. You are happy with yourself, your personal relationships are great and you love your meaningful work. (If you have followed this strategy through so far, it *is* possible!) You have already begun to find yourself automatically looking outwards more and thinking about a way of making an increased contribution to the wider world. But do you know where to start? In these days of mass media it is so easy to feel overwhelmed by the competing needs of our increasingly globalized community. It is understandable that many people end up taking the easiest and quickest option. This could be a prod to their conscience by glancing at a clever advert, or a chance hearing of a personal story that echoed their own.

As I write this, I am aware that I have pressed one of my own buttons. So here's a relevant confession!

I spent most of my childhood unhappily in children's homes. Throughout my adult life I talked frequently about how, one day, I wanted to help children in care have a better quality of life. But it was not until two years ago, when one of my editors made it so easy for me to act, that I did anything remotely useful for these seriously disadvantaged children. She asked a charity that had been set up to help such children to make contact with me. Although, for the moment, I am doing much less than I would like to do, I know that I am making a special contribution by being someone who can talk first-hand about the experience of being in care. When I offered this help, I had no idea that it could be so rewarding for me. Publicly sharing some of my experiences also started my brother and myself talking (and healing) in a way that we had never been able to do before (I will ease my guilt a little by using this opportunity to tell you that the charity is called 'The Who Cares Trust' and that their excellent work is described on their website: www.thewhocarestrust.org.uk).

But choosing how to make a *meaningful* and *well-targeted* contribution of our time, effort, money or influence is an important decision. We should not wait for a knee-jerk response to do that for us – even if it should send us in the perfect direction. I hope these exercises will help you to clarify the best way for you to give your life more meaning and purpose by becoming more able to be of significant service to the wider community in which you live.

Knowing we are a caring person is good for our inner peace of mind, but acting in a constructively caring manner is even better and it can bring many other unexpected rewards.

To know even one life has breathed easier because you have lived. This is to have succeeded.

RALPH WALDO EMERSON

Action time!

- **Over the next week, note down some world issues and problems which are of interest to you.** Scan the papers and cut out stories that move you. Alternatively (or as well) look through the listings in a digest of charities or pressure or action groups. (But remember that the ideal one might not yet exist – you may have to start it!) Choose two or three which you would like to make a contribution (or further contribution) towards.

- **Make a list of skills you currently possess which could be of help to others** (for example, typing / listening / bookkeeping / computer systems / management / conflict resolution / writing / publicity, and so forth).

- **Make a note of some key examples of personal wisdom that you have gathered from successfully overcoming problems and transitions in your own life.** (For example, giving up smoking / parenting / illness / dealing with a burglary / bereavement / early retirement / redundancy / pressurizing local government over environmental issues / harassment, and so forth.)

- **Look at your diary and reflect calmly on exactly how much time you have available to offer.** (Remember it is kinder and wiser to err on the side of under-committing at first.)

- **Reflect on your current financial position and assess whether you could afford to donate money.**

- **Note any other resources you have which could be of help** (for example, a computer / a spare room / books / a pram / old clothes / office space / staff time, and so forth).

- **Use the internet or the library (ask for help – it will usually be willingly given) to research organizations which might be able to help you to make your contribution.** Talk freely with friends and colleagues about what you are doing – I find that almost always someone knows someone who knows someone who can help.

- **Write or ring these organizations outlining any relevant skills and personal wisdom and resources you have to offer.** (They will welcome your well-thought-through approach.) Be very clear with them about the amount of time you might be able to commit.

Let's be kinder to each other.

ALDOUS HUXLEY'S LAST WORDS

STEP 15

Strengthen your connection with nature

This step will obviously be more important for some of you than others. But, nevertheless, I have not yet met anyone, even amongst the hardened devotees of metropolitan life, who cannot benefit from making a stronger connection with the natural world. Even modern town planners and road and property developers have at last got the message! They have learned the hard way (in my country at least) that efficiency and economy are not enough to please their public. They now know they must provide trees, not just the odd sad-looking plant, within their office buildings and apartment blocks, and that they must put flowers, and not just plastic bollards, in the centre of their roads. People have demanded these often expensive and inconvenient natural additions to their urban

environments because they have felt the dehumanizing effect of living without them.

Similar interesting changes are taking place in the countryside as well. In almost all developed countries (and many others as well), people are questioning many of the 'improvements' to land cultivation of the last century. This is not just because they may threaten the future of the planet and poison us with too many pesticides, but because people have complained that they have stopped them and their children being able to be in such intimate contact with the natural world. So we are seeing wire fences being replaced by old-fashioned hedges, footpaths being reopened and more and more land being left to grow wild.

But are these kinds of communal changes enough for you? Are you perhaps craving for more hands-on contact with nature? Maybe the hectic rush of trying to balance many different demands on your life to achieve this would seem like an impossible dream. Maybe you have settled happily for buying a CD of bird song sounds and artificial flowers that don't need watering, and have laid a concrete lawn that doesn't need cutting. If so, skip this step and turn to Step 16. But those of you who still yearn for more might find it helpful to do the following exercises.

Take the time to savour and appreciate the natural world around you.

A human being is part of a whole, called by us the 'universe', a part limited in time and space. He experiences himself, his thoughts and feelings, as something separated from the rest – a kind of optical delusion of his consciousness ... Our task must be to free ourselves from this prison by widening our circle of compassion to embrace all living creatures and the whole of nature in its beauty.

ALBERT EINSTEIN

Action time!

- **Over the next week increase your contact with nature by doing the following** (or indeed anything else that you can think of yourself):

  - make a conscious effort to set aside a few moments at different points in the day to savour and appreciate the natural world around you. Try to imagine that you are a new visitor to your area. My eyes were reopened to many beautiful details in our wet, windy, green English surroundings last year when some visitors from a dry desert-style land visited us. (For example, notice the health and growth of your house plants – even talk to them if you are that way inclined! Be more aware of the sky – watch the movement of any clouds and birds and notice the rise of the moon and the appearance of the stars; stop to smell the scent of flowers or grass; spend more time in close contact with your pets or notice and appreciate the variety of other animals and insects you see as you travel around; look for, draw or collect as many varieties of leaves as you can.)

– buy or pick yourself a carefully selected bunch of flowers and green foliage. Doing this will focus your attention more on the different varieties, shapes and shades. (You could resolve to make this a regular treat.)

– plant some quick sprouting beans or seeds (cress would do) or put a cutting in a jar of water. Place this in a position where you can watch and reflect on the growth of new plant life *every* day. (For example, on the kitchen windowsill or beside your desk.)

- **After this week, reflect on the impact that giving yourself some extra contact with nature had on you.** If it was beneficial, ask yourself how you can ensure that you have more. (For example, walk part of the way to work; prioritize visits to the countryside or sea, or set a regular time for outings such as once a month; plan to redesign your garden or replant your window box; buy a book on bird watching or build a bird table; hold staff meetings in gardens; treat yourself to an outdoor heater and ski jacket so you can take a drink or meal outside even in winter; take time to admire the flowers that burst through the concrete of paths, and so forth.)

I like trees because they seem more resigned to the way they have to live than other things do.

WILLA CATHER

And finally . . .

STEP 16

Check you are balancing your life to suit your wants and needs

During the last few months, innumerable people, on hearing the title of this book, have said, *'Oh, great. Exactly what I need – tips on how to balance my life.'* But I hope by now you have realized that I believe there is so much more to 'getting a life' than learning the art of juggling the different 'balls' in our current lives. In fact, I believe that for people who **build** and **maintain** a life around the principles I have suggested in this book, life balance is rarely ever an issue. This is because the moment they sense that their lifestyle is beginning to stop them getting what they *want* and *need* they take corrective action. Perhaps this is because once you have had a quality life you are never again prepared to settle for anything less. It is a wonderfully rewarding part of my job to see people who once felt so powerless and who

used to exude cynicism and depression, being fiercely protective of their right to be happy and lead meaningful, well-balanced lives.

If you have worked through the exercises and suggestions in this book, you too should have *begun to* taste the fruits of your efforts. You should be:

- more confident in your ability to meet your own and your dependants' survival needs for the foreseeable future
- already benefiting from your new self-nurturing habits and be excited about the future you have planned for yourself
- feeling less lonely and having more fun and stimulating social experiences
- finding your work more satisfying and easier to manage
- feeling more 'at one' with the wider world and proud of the contribution you are making in your community.

If you are not, don't panic. You haven't failed. You are not a 'hopeless case'. It is just that you have probably arrived at this section a little too soon. Perhaps you need to do some more work in one or more of the four arenas. But if your curiosity insists you read on now, please do bear in mind that this section is primarily intended for those who are nearer 'the finishing post' of this strategy than you are at this moment in time.

• • • • • • • • •

Imagine for a moment that over the last couple of months you have devoted much of your precious time and energy (and some money) to landscaping a garden. You have taken immense care to ensure that it is the kind that is ecologically balanced. It is filled (but not overfilled!) with a wide variety of interesting and beautiful plants. It is relaxing to be in and no longer fills you with guilt the moment you look around it. You also feel extremely relieved knowing that you have made sure that it will stay that way. (You have carefully chosen a style that is well within your capabilities to maintain.)

As you can still vividly recall the jungle (or wasteland) it once was, wouldn't you be more than willing to put in a little more energy to observe and tend to it in this 'make or break' stage of its young growth? I am sure you would because you would have faith in its ability to repay your efforts a thousand fold in the not-too-distant future.

This is exactly the approach I hope you will now adopt towards the nurturing of your fledgling new life. **Eventually your life will become largely self-balancing, but for the next few months many of the changes and new habits that you have adopted will be as fragile as new seedlings – they too will need some careful monitoring.** But, as with your new garden, your life-maintenance work should now be much quicker and easier to do. If it is done regularly, its balance will be easily maintained because you will ensure that unwanted 'weeds' don't take root and it doesn't become suffocatingly 'over-grown'.

But, of course, however diligent a 'gardener' you are, your new life will always be at risk from sabotaging 'storms' and 'infections' that are beyond your control. These could come from forces within your 'garden' (such as unexpected illness or bereavement) or they could come from the wider world (such as a world crisis). As I am writing this, in the autumn of 2001, millions of people's lives are being drastically affected by what is now described as 'An International War on Terrorism'.

So occasionally you may have to turn your 'garden' upside down again, revisit this strategy and do some major reorganization. But, generally speaking, a monthly inspection and a small amount of 'weeding', 'pruning' and 'planting' should keep your life in a highly manageable and well-balanced state from now on.

Eventually your life-maintenance will become another set of well-established good life-habits. You will routinely observe your own progress and readjust your lifestyle (more often than not without even being consciously aware that you have gone into 'conservation mode'). But initially you may need to make sure that such reviewing happens by scheduling in an odd hour or two each month in your diary. The suggestions in the following 'Action Time!' section should help to speed up the task and ensure that it is done thoroughly.

If you can find someone else to team up with to do this work, it can be more effective and even become very pleasurable. Many of my clients have done this very successfully. They have agreed to meet up with a friend regularly for lunch or an evening drink. But remember that if you are going to do this, be sure to programme in some life-balancing review time for each person *before* the fun starts!

It is your everyday choices about how to use your time and energy that will balance or unbalance your life.

Action time!

- **You can use the following questions as an initial framework for your self-reflection.** But after three months or so, you may want to create your own checklist. Keep your question list as short and simple as you can (then you are more likely to use it!). Soon you will not need to even use a list to prompt your thinking – asking yourself these kinds of questions will have become a habit.

  Put a tick in the box at the side of any questions to indicate that those areas may need some attention.

1. The essential foundations – re-evaluating your survival needs

– Have there been any external changes which have affected my ability to meet my basic survival needs? (For example, loss of income / unexpected bills / sharp rise in interest rates / new commitments such as an extra child or a new car.) ☐

- Have I been keeping a realistic perspective on this area of my life or have I been unduly worrying? ☐

2. Nurturing your body, mind and spirit

- Have I been giving my body adequate care and attention? (For example, enough rest / a nurturing diet.) ☐
- Have I been keeping up with my anti-stress routines? (For example, regular meditation / exercise.) ☐
- Am I satisfied with my own personal development over the past month? (For example, am I stretching my potential and stimulating my creativity and learning or just merely vegetating or getting by?) ☐
- Have I changed my ideas about what I want in relation to my life-dream? ☐
- Have I given myself enough fun and pleasurable sensations? ☐
- Have I been feeding my spirit well enough? ☐
- Have I been true to my principles and values? ☐

3. Developing a happy and fulfilling personal life

- Have I got what I need from my intimate relationships? ☐
- Have I contributed as much as I could to my intimate relationships? ☐
- Have I had a good-enough social life? ☐
- Are any of my friendships in need of attention? ☐

4. Finding satisfaction at work

- Have I been enjoying my work enough? ☐
- Has my work been purposeful and meaningful enough? ☐
- Have I managed to maintain a positive outlook when I have been under pressure? ☐
- Do any of my working relationships need attention? ☐

5. Connecting with the wider world

- Have I made a good-enough contribution to the community in which I live? ☐
- Have I given myself enough contact with nature? ☐

- **Take some time to reflect on what you may need to do next month in the areas which you have marked as in need of attention.** Decide upon some resolutions, but limit yourself to three for any one section. (Otherwise you may overload yourself and undo all your previous good work.)

- **Take five different coloured pens to write your resolution list in order of priority.** (Use a different colour for each of the five areas, for example, a red pen for your 're-evaluating your survival needs' resolutions; a blue pen for your 'connecting with the wider world' resolutions, and so forth.) Prioritizing may be difficult to do, and you could find your resolutions fighting with each other for your time and energy. For example, *'Should I spend this evening checking my bank statements'* (survival needs) or *'Should I go out to the quiz show at the pub where I might meet some friends'* (personal life). Remember these everyday choices may not seem that significant at the time, but they are crucial in terms of the overall balance of your life.

- **Pin up your coloured prioritized list in a prominent position where you (and others) will be reminded of it daily.** This will help you to make the choices you need to make in order to keep the balance in your life that you currently want and need.

- **When you do your review next month, start by reflecting on this list.** Ask yourself if each resolution has been achieved satisfactorily. If some have not been, ask yourself if you sabotaged them by not allocating them enough time and energy. Decide whether or not they need to be moved further up your priority list next month. Using the coloured pens will help you to see whether one area of your life is being over or under-prioritized on a regular basis. If this happens, you will then know that you must go 'back to the drawing board' and do a more thorough review. You could perhaps read this book again to help you see what changes you could make.

Enjoy your new life!

You have now reinvented your life, if not yourself as well! A very large part of you should be feeling excited and optimistic about the future. However, you wouldn't be human if there wasn't a negative demon hiding within you as well. Of course there will be times when you will feel scared about some of the changes you are making. As we have acknowledged several times in this book, 'getting a life' is a challenging business, especially in a world where so many people are 'selling out' on their human right to achieve this.

So make sure that you mix with as many POSITIVE and HAPPY people as you can during the next few months. Stick fast to those friends, relatives and colleagues who believe you can do it. (The others can have your altruistic attention later.) Don't hold back on asking for their support when you need it. If you have had the motivation to read this far, trust that this is a crucial turning point in your life. Go for it with confidence! And, I hope you have fun while you do.

Further help

Recommended reading

Richard Nelson Bolles, *What Colour Is Your Parachute? A Practical Manual for Job Hunters and Career-Changers* (Ten Speed Press, 2000)

Richard Carlson, *Don't Sweat the Small Stuff – and It's All Small Stuff* (Hyperion, 1998)

Marilyn Diamond, *Fitonics for Life: Mind and Body Fitness for a High-Energy Lifestyle* (Thorsons, 1998)

Stephanie Dowrick, *The Universal Heart: Golden Rules for Golden Relationships* (Penguin, 2001)

John Gray, *How to Get What You Want and Want What You Have* (Vermillion, 2001)

Susan Jeffers, *Dare to Connect: How to Create Confidence, Trust and Loving Relationships* (Piatkus, 1995)

Robert Holden, *Shift Happens: Powerful Ways to Transform Your Life* (Hodder and Stoughton, 2000)

Leslie Kenton, *Ten Steps to a Younger You* (Vermillion, 2000)

Joel Levey and Michelle Levey, *Living in Balance: A Dynamic Approach for Creating Harmony and Wholeness in a Chaotic World* (Conari Press, 1998)

Gael Lindenfield, *Assert Yourself* (Thorsons, 1986)

___, *Super Confidence* (Thorsons, 1989)

___, *The Positive Woman* (Thorsons, 1992)

___, *Managing Anger* (Thorsons, 1993)

___, *Self Esteem* (Thorsons, 1995)

___, *Self Motivation* (Thorsons, 1996)

___, *Emotional Confidence* (Thorsons, 1997)

___, *Success from Setbacks* (Thorsons, 1999)

___, *Confident Children* (Thorsons, 2000)

___, *Confident Teens* (Thorsons, 2001)

___, *Shortcuts to Bouncing Back from Heartbreak* (Thorsons, 2002)

___, *Shortcuts to Making Hard Choices Easy* (Thorsons, 2002)

Gael Lindenfield and Malcolm Vandenburg, *Positive Under Pressure* (Thorsons, 2000)

Ann McGee-Cooper, et al, *You Don't Have to Go Home from Work Exhausted! A Program to Bring Joy, Energy and Balance to Your Life* (Bantam Books, 1992)

Julie Morganstern, *Organizing from Inside Out* (Hodder and Stoughton, 2000)

Susan Quilliam, *Love Coach* (Thorsons, 2000)

Cheryl Richardson, *Take Time for Your Life: A Seven-Step Programme for Creating the Life You Want* (Bantam, 2000)

Dr Brian Roet, *The Confidence to Be Yourself: How to Boost Your Self-Esteem* (Piatkus, 1998)

John-Roger and Peter McWilliams, *Do It! A Guide to Living Your Dreams* (Thorsons, 1992)

Useful internet sites

The following sites could be helpful to readers in the UK. Other readers may want to search for local sites. You can initiate a search by just entering the words Work + Life or Life + Balance.

www.ivillage.co.uk/workcareer/worklife

This site is a web community for women. It offers tips on work-life balance issues, including childcare options, working from home, setting up your own business, networking and family-friendly firms.

www.flametree.co.uk

A specialist consultancy offering advice to individuals and organizations on work-life issues. Includes many inspiring ideas for managing your home more efficiently, including imaginative ways to do this through using web services.

www.parentsatwork.org.uk

This organization acts as a voice of the working parent. Advises on latest research, employment rights, benefits and career leave. Campaigns on behalf of parents with special problems, such as parenting children with disabilities and being a single parent.

www.dfee.gov.uk/work-lifebalance

A government site offering useful information on benefits and legal position. Publishes and undertakes research, and promotes good employment practice and childcare support schemes.

Cassettes

Gael Lindenfield has made a number of personal-development tapes. Each is designed as a self-help programme of exercises to be used on a regular basis. The list of titles includes:

Self Motivation (Thorsons, 1997)
Self Esteem (Thorsons, 1998)
Success from Setbacks (Thorsons, 1999)
Managing Emotions at Work (Thorsons, 1999)
Emotional Confidence (Thorsons, 2000)

These cassettes are available at all good bookshops, or direct from Thorsons (telephone 0870 900 2050 or 0141 306 3296).

About the author

You can contact Gael Lindenfield through her publishers at the following address:

Gael Lindenfield c/o Thorsons
HarperCollins*Publishers*
77–85 Fulham Palace Road
Hammersmith
London W6 8JB
United Kingdom

Or you can contact her directly by email: lindenfield.office@btinternet.com

For further information about Gael Lindenfield and her current programme, go to her website:

www.gael-lindenfield.com